UNMOVABLE

A 14-Day Devotional For The Unmovable Woman

NADINE VALENTINE

DAYELight
PUBLISHERS

ISBN: 978-1-949343-90-8

Acknowledgments

I give total honor to the Lord Jesus Christ, who has redeemed me from a life filled with hopelessness, despair, and brokenness. Because He lives, I now face a bright tomorrow and I can smile knowing that my Redeemer lives, and I will live with Him forever.

I also give honor to my husband, Michael, for his constant love, encouragement, and support and for always reminding me that I should believe in the gifts and abilities that God has placed in me.

I also want to thank Yvane Carty, who encouraged me to start writing, Evelyn Anderson, my sisters: Shirley and Moreen, and my mother: Mrs. Delsy Chisholm, who always supports and cheers me on.

Table of Contents

Introduction

I was inspired to write this devotional to encourage those of us who have known what it is to survive and overcome great personal failures, setbacks, and rejections. It was written as a companion to "Unmovable: Victory Despite the Storms." This devotional will uplift your heart with daily Scripture verses and encourage you as you go through your day.

There are 14 daily verses, with inspirational illustrations and relevant questions for each day's challenges and victories.

I pray you will be challenged to remain unmovable as you walk with the Lord in the light of His Word.

"And Mary said, My soul doth magnify the Lord, and my spirit hath rejoiced in God my Saviour." (Luke 1:46-47).

Mary woke up one morning, thinking it was going to be a normal day as usual but before that day ended, she was impregnated with the seed of God that would result in the Son of God coming to earth to dwell among men. Have you ever been in a situation where everything you planned got thrown through the window and your whole life was redirected?

Many of us, like Mary, have experienced that same situation but not all of us responded like her, I am sure. In fact, many would argue that God was asking too much of them, but Mary's initial response to the angel in Luke 1:38 and her response in song when she visited Elizabeth, shows that God did not make a mistake when He chose her.

She submitted and she rejoiced. She did not argue, get depressed or throw tantrums. She knew her life was never going to be the same again, but she submitted, and rejoiced that God had chosen her for such an honor. She remained unmovable and steadfast in her love and devotion for the Lord and became known as the mother of the Lord Jesus.

Daily Reflection:

In what areas do you need to submit to the Lord?

_____

_____

_____

_____

Daily Prayer:

Lord, forgive me for the times I have not submitted to Your will for my life. Help me to surrender and be obedient to all that You have called me to do. Teach me how to rejoice and be glad for all that You do for and through me, in Jesus Name. Amen.

Day 2

"The woman saith unto him, Sir, give me this water, that I thirst not, neither come hither to draw." (John 4:15).

I grew up in Jamaica where it is summer all year round. It does get cool or cold, depending on which part of the island you are from. Our island is blessed with cool rivers, amazing waterfalls, and beautiful beaches. We are an island, so we are surrounded by water.

When I was growing up, many homes did not have water being piped to their homes. If there was a river or a public pipe, that was where you would often see kids and adults lined up to catch water in their containers. Water is a precious commodity, and, in many third world countries, many people struggle to even have clean drinking water.

In John 4, when Jesus meets the woman at the well, she was getting water at a time when other women were home. Bible scholars have posited that she did this because she was living a sinful lifestyle, so to escape the gossip and the scorn from the other women, she went to the well before they did. Whatever the reason for being at the well at that time, she met Someone who spoke to her situation and gave her what she REALLY needed. Like many of us she was looking for a temporary fix for a condition that needed an eternal solution. How many times do we go through life, seeking fulfillment in all the wrong places with all the wrong people? The Lord alone knows our true needs and is ready to give you what you REALLY need.

Daily Reflection:

If you could have anything from the Lord today, what would that be?

_____

_____

_____

_____

_____

Daily Prayer:

Lord, teach me to seek what is eternal and trust in You to supply all my needs. Amen.

Day 3

"And Sarah said, God hath made me to laugh, so that all that hear will laugh with me." (Genesis 21:6).

How many of us know what it is like to be in some dark places, where there is literally no light shining through? As I am typing this, I have my cell phone's flashlight on because I needed to see something and really did not want to get up and turn on the room light. What a difference the light made. What I could not see before became illuminated and I could continue my reading.

Sarah must have had a similar experience at the birth of Isaac. For years she watched every other woman around her enjoy the pleasure of holding a baby in their arms, while hers remained empty. She must have endured so much hurt and disappointment because of this missing part of her life. But God had not forgotten her, had He? One day, her weeping turned into joy and she laughed.

She laughed because God had kept His promises to His servants from a year earlier. She laughed because He had lifted her head and taken away her bareness. She laughed because she was now a mother of a son. Finally, her dream had become a reality.

That is how it is for many of us when the darkness of our past becomes illuminated by the light of our todays. We can laugh again because truly He who promised to make a way or provide or heal, did exactly as He said He would do.

Daily Reflection:

Like Sarah, can you laugh at something the Lord did solely for you?

_____

_____

_____

_____

_____

_____

_____

_____

Daily Prayer:

Dear Lord, thank You for turning my sorrow into joy. Thank You for causing me to laugh again. All that You promised to do, You have done, and I rejoice at the works of Your hands. Amen.

Day 4

"And Hannah prayed, and said, My heart rejoiceth in the Lord, mine horn is exalted in the Lord: my mouth is enlarged over mine enemies; because I rejoice in thy salvation." (1 Samuel 2:1).

I remember as a student dealing with some challenging situations. I was often bullied and called names because I was slight and skinny. That made me extremely self-conscious about my look/image. In fact, I struggled with my self-esteem for years and always admired those who seem to have it together more than I did. After coming into a personal relationship with Jesus Christ, He taught me, through His Word, that my validation did not come from another mortal like myself but from Him and, skinny and all, I was precious and fearfully and wonderfully made. Many women now pay money to be petite and slender, something that I never thought possible.

Hannah dealt with similar issues of her own because of her inability to conceive and bare her husband children. His other wife did not make the situation any better with her constant gloating and bullying attitude. All of that changed one day for Hannah, however, when the God of Israel, through Eli the prophet, spoke an on-time word to her and she conceived and bore Samuel. Nothing was ever heard of Penninah and her children, but Samuel went on to become Israel's judge and prophet and Hannah would also be blessed with five more children.

When God turns things around, He does it in fine style, as Hannah would later testify (See 1 Samuel 2:1-10).

Daily Reflection:

Can you identify one way in which the Lord has vindicated you?

_____

_____

_____

_____

_____

Daily Prayer:

Lord, thank You that You hear and answer prayers. Thank You that You are touched with the feelings of our infirmities and You hurt when we hurt and cry when we cry. Thank You that You are our Vindicator and our Righteous Judge, always and forevermore. Amen.

"The Lord is my shepherd; I shall not want." (Psalm 23:1).

When life gets you down, it is so wonderful to know that you are not alone and there is a God who cares about you. At the end of it all, we are sheep and our Lord is the Shepherd of our souls. He knows when we are up; He knows when we are down. He knows every little thing there is to know about us, even the things we tend to hide from those around us.

David knew the shepherd life very well because he started life as a shepherd tending to his father's flock. He knew the tendency of sheep to wander off and get lost, if there was no one to guide them. He knew that sometimes you would have stragglers who needed to be carefully monitored and he also knew that predators were never far from the flock. These predators waited for opportunities to steal and kill the flock. As a shepherd, it was important to stay awake and watch over the flock and get them to safety when the weather was not pleasant.

As believers, we are tended to in the same way by our heavenly Father. He never sleeps nor slumbers and He keeps watch over His flock to ensure that all are safe. He protects us from the enemy of our souls, and He will leave the ninety and nine to go look for the one sheep that gets lost.

I am reminded of this timeless hymn, **Savior, Like a Shepherd Lead Us,** and its comforting words: *"Savior, like a shepherd lead us, Much we need thy tender care."* This is so needed in our world today as technology increases and our world gets so noisier and busier. We need to be reminded of this one truth: the Lord is our Shepherd; we shall not want.

Daily Reflection:

In what way is the Lord a Shepherd to you?

_____

_____

_____

_____

_____

Daily Prayer:

Lord, thank You for being the Shepherd of my soul. Thank You for leading me to quiet waters so I can rest in You. Thank You for providing all I want in this life and the one to come. Thank You for protecting me from all that would harm me. Amen.

Day 6

"The Lord hath appeared of old unto me, saying, Yea, I have loved thee with an everlasting love: therefore, with lovingkindness have I drawn thee." (Jeremiah 31:3).

The nation of Judah was in a state of great apostasy, with sure judgment awaiting them, but the Lord's love was still available for anyone who would turn to Him. He had sent prophet after prophet to warn them about their coming exile, but they were unwilling to turn to the God of their salvation. In as much as their exile was prophesied, so too was their eventual return to Jerusalem and restoration to the God of their fathers.

God's justice and holiness are integral aspects of His divine nature. Therefore, sin must be punished, but His merciful and compassionate nature also leaves room for restoration and reconciliation. No matter how far we have gone in sin, God's love will always be available to us, if we want it. John 3:16 reminds us of God's love for the world that He created, and it is His desire that all men come to the saving knowledge of the Lord Jesus Christ (See 1 Timothy 2:4). Be encouraged that no matter where you and I are on the path of life, God's love is always available to those who want it.

Daily Reflection:

What are some of the ways in which you have experienced God's restoration and love?

_____

_____

_____

_____

_____

Daily Prayer:

Lord, thank You for loving me with an everlasting love. I know I have sinned against You so many times but still You love me. Teach me to love You and obey Your Word, so I can be with You always. Amen.

Day 7

"She said, No man, Lord. And Jesus said unto her, Neither do I condemn thee: go, and sin no more." (John 8:11).

One of the most interesting things about Jesus' encounter with this woman is the fact that no one was apparently ever caught with her. For those of us who know better, she was not guilty of committing adultery by herself; there must have been another guilty party, yet she was the only one brought to Jesus.

The intention of the religious leaders was really to catch Jesus off-guard and accuse Him, but the Son of God was so very much aware of what His enemies were planning. His writing on the ground has made us wonder, "What could He have possibly been writing?" We will never know on this side of heaven but whatever He wrote, it made those who were ready to stone the woman change their minds and leave. What is ironic about this account is that the One who could condemn her to death and throw her in hell, showed her the most mercy when He said, *"Neither do I condemn thee, go, and sin no more."*

The Lord said He never came to condemn the world but to save the world (See John 3:17) and His desire is for none to perish but for all to have everlasting life. This is good news for many who believe that it is too late for them because they have sinned too much. Jesus came to save us from our sins. He did not come to destroy men's lives but to save them (See Luke 9:56).

Daily Reflection:

Can you remember a time when the Lord showed great compassion to you?

_____

_____

_____

_____

_____

Daily Prayer:

Lord, thank You for coming into this world to save men from their sins. We would be lost and undone without You. Your love is so amazing and because of this love we can overcome the ravages of sin. Thank You for being the Savior of the world. Amen.

"I will bless the Lord at all times: his praise shall continually be in my mouth." (Psalm 34:1).

David knew what it was to endure serious opposition and persecution, as well as betrayal and heartbreak. He also knew what it was to break God's law and live with the consequences of his sins. Yet, this man after God's own heart could emphatically declare that he would be intentional about praising his God, "at all times."

All of us can relate to challenging, difficult times when praising God was probably the most difficult thing to do, but it is in these times that we must learn to offer up a sacrifice of praise to the King of kings and the Lord of lords.

At the time of this writing, our world is being pummeled by a deadly virus. Many lives have been lost and the world has been disrupted on every level. For those of us who believe in the Lord

Jesus Christ, we know this virus does not have the last word. Our God has the final say, and He is still greater than anything that comes against us. So, like David, we declare, without apology, that, "We will bless the Lord at all times. His praise shall continually be in our mouths."

Daily Reflection:

Can you identify a specific time when you had to give the Lord a "sacrifice of praise?"

_____

_____

_____

_____

_____

Daily Prayer:

Lord, thank You for the times when You enabled me, by Your Spirit, to give You a sacrifice of praise. By being intentional about praising You in the rough times, I have learned how to truly bless you. Amen.

Day 9

"O our God, wilt thou not judge them? for we have no might against this great company that cometh against us; neither know we what to do: but our eyes are upon thee." (2 Chronicles 20:12).

King Jehoshaphat was in a crisis. He was about to be overrun by three mighty armies from three nations. The little nation of Judah was no match for the armies of Moab, Ammon, and Mount Seir. The king, however, did the only thing he knew; he called for a fast throughout the land and gathered all the cities of Judah together to seek the Lord.

What is admirable about the king is that he did not look to the arm of flesh to provide the help he knew he was going to need; he looked for divine help. He sought the Lord in prayer and fasting. After this, the Word of the Lord came through the mouth of the prophet, Jahaziel (See 2 Chronicles 20:15-17).

This man of God knew where his help came from. He did not look to man, the stars, or false prophets. He looked to the One who sits in heaven. Because King Jehoshaphat enquired of the Lord, he got the victory over the enemies of Judah. As many as they were, they were no match for the might and power of almighty God. Truly the battle belongs to the Lord.

Daily Reflection:

Can you remember a time when everything was against you, but God stepped in and gave you the victory because you sought Him in prayer and fasting?

_____

_____

_____

_____

_____

Daily Prayer:

Lord, thank You for being a mighty Warrior. Thank You that the battle belongs to You and

nothing or no one can stand against the God who reigns above. Thank You that when I put my trust in You, I will always have the victory. Amen.

"David said moreover, The Lord that delivered me out of the paw of the lion, and out of the paw of the bear, he will deliver me out of the hand of this Philistine. And Saul said unto David, Go, and the Lord be with thee." (1 Samuel 17:37).

David was a boy when he encountered the giant from Gath, Goliath. He, however, knew that because God was with him, he was undefeatable. David never second-guessed or wavered in his faith in God. He knew he was going to kill Goliath, even though all he had was a slingshot. The giant had the armor, spear, javelin, and the bow, but David had a big God who never lost a battle. David knew his God and knew He had his back.

When we are in a fight for our lives, we need to know who has our back. We need to remember that God promises never to leave us nor forsake us. He promises to be with us to the end. Despite our trials and circumstances, we serve a God who is well able to deliver us from evil (See Matthew 6:13) and to keep us from falling (See Jude 24).

David knew that despite his size and threats, Goliath was like an ant to the God who parted the Red Sea and defeated mighty nations with just the breath of His mouth. David knew this giant would fall before the God who thundered from heaven and roared upon the waters.

When we know our God, the impossible becomes possible and the giant will fall.

Daily Reflection:

Do you remember a time when God delivered you from a "giant?"

_____

_____

_____

_____

_____

Daily Prayer:

Lord Jesus, thank You for delivering us from giants who come to intimidate us and drive fear into us. Thank You that no weapon formed against us shall prosper. You are a big and mighty God who can do more than we can ask or think. Amen.

"The Lord is merciful and gracious, slow to anger, and plenteous in mercy." (Psalm 103:8).

So many times, we find ourselves in situations where we struggle to forgive ourselves for the things we did in our past. We sometimes find it hard to forgive those who have hurt us, but it is the Lord's will for us to walk in forgiveness and healing. The Lord, who is merciful, wants us to show mercy and He wants us to forgive those who hurt us.

You may say it is too hard to move past that situation but with God it is possible. In order to be forgiven, we must forgive others and ourselves. He is still the balm in Gilead. He is still the God who turns our wailing to dancing.

The mercies of the Lord are new every morning. His anger only lasts for a while, but His mercy is everlasting. God is a God of restoration and healing and He has great plans for His people. No matter where we have been or what we have done, God's mercy is extended to us every day.

Daily Reflection:

Are you struggling to forgive yourself or someone else?

_____

_____

_____

_____

_____

Daily Prayer:

Lord, teach me to forgive myself and others. Thank You that You are a God of mercy and grace and Your anger does not last always. Thank You, Lord, that Your mercies are new every morning. Amen.

"Trust in the Lord with all thine heart; and lean not unto thine own understanding. In all thy ways acknowledge him, and he shall direct thy paths." *(Proverbs 3:5-6).*

Trusting in the Lord requires that we not lean to our own understanding. As human beings we often want to rationalize and explain things away, but the truth is, we must learn to walk by faith and not by sight when we are in covenant relationship with the living God. His ways are high above ours as well as His thoughts (See Isaiah 55:8).

When we make decisions, without seeking the Lord's will, we run the risk of walking in disobedience and out of His will. The Scriptures encourage us to seek God's will first, so everything we need can be added to our lives (See Matthew 6:33).

Being in a relationship with the Lord means that we are expected to have the Lord's direction for every step of our lives. Some may struggle with this, but if we do not adhere to this Biblical principle, we can become self-willed and rebellious like King Saul. See 1 Samuel for his story that did not end well. Let us endeavor to walk in obedience and trust the Lord to guide us along life's path. He knows the end from the beginning (See Isaiah 46:10) and He knows what is best for us.

Daily Reflection:

Can you identify a time when you struggled to choose God's will over yours?

_____

_____

_____

_____

_____

Daily Prayer:

Lord, thank You that You know what is best for me. Help me to know Your will and be obedient to it. Help me to walk by faith always. Amen.

"To appoint unto them that mourn in Zion, to give unto them beauty for ashes..." (Isaiah 61:3a).

I saiah prophesied to the children of Israel that a time was coming when everything they had lost would be restored. I can testify that God is truly a Restorer because I have seen Him do it in the lives of broken people. Remember Mary who had seven demons cast out of her? (See Luke 8:2). Remember the woman at the well who was living a sinful lifestyle? (See John 4).

There are people who have wasted many years of their lives in sin and never thought they could ever do anything for God, but He can take the broken pieces of their lives and put them back together again in a beautiful way. Jesus told His disciples that what is impossible with man, is possible with God (See Luke 18:27).

He came to destroy the works of the devil (See 1 John 3:8) and save that which was lost (See Luke

19:10). He also came to set the captives free (See Luke 4:18) so all we need to do is surrender it all to Jesus and watch Him do what He does best: heal and restore the broken.

Daily Reflection:

Identify one area of your life where you have experienced God's complete restoration and healing?

_____

_____

_____

_____

_____

Daily Prayer:

Lord, thank You for healing and restoring the broken pieces of our lives. Thank You for taking our ashes and giving us Your beauty so You can be glorified. Amen.

Day 14

"Fear not: for I have redeemed thee, I have called thee by thy name; thou art mine." (Isaiah 43:1B).

The Lord calls us His own. It is so comforting to know that when we become children of God, we join a family that crosses all ethnic, racial, cultural, and geographical lines. We are joined and knitted together by the blood of Jesus. We can all collectively address the Lord God as Abba, our Father, along with the Jews. Jesus, because of His finished work on Calvary, has made one new man (See Ephesians 2:14-16).

We may not understand it now, but we are completely reconciled back to the Father and called His own. We are now seated in heavenly places with Christ Jesus our Lord (See Ephesians 2:6). We are children of the King.

We are His masterpiece, saved for good works (See Ephesians 2:10). We are redeemed by the blood of the Lamb (See Ephesians 1:7) and have a living hope. We are no longer destined for an eternity without Jesus, but we will be with Him forevermore. What a glorious future we have awaiting us!

Daily Reflection:

What are you looking forward to the most when Jesus returns?

_____

_____

_____

_____

_____

Daily Prayer:

Lord, thank You for the living hope we have in You. If it were not for You, where would we be? Thank You for giving Your Life, so I can live with You for all eternity. Amen.

About the Author

Nadine Valentine is a native of Jamaica who currently resides in sunny Florida. Growing up in rural Jamaica, she always enjoyed reading and writing stories in school. Over time that evolved into journal writing, which she still does as time allows. An avid reader, she has an interest in books that inspire and motivate others to grow. Her favorite book is the Bible, from which she has grown her own faith and has birthed in her a desire to write books that help to strengthen Christian women to grow their faith in God despite the trials of life.

Nadine's favorite Scripture is: "I can do all things through Christ who strengthens me." (Philippians 4:13). She walks out this Scripture in her own life. She believes that with God all things are possible. She has overcome molestation, domestic violence, physical abuse, emotional trauma, verbal abuse, sexual abuse, and divorce through the life-changing power of the Word of God.

She is now a wife, mom, ordained minister, gospel recording artist and author who maintains that "only what I do for Christ will last."

www.ingramcontent.com/pod-product-compliance
Lightning Source LLC
Chambersburg PA
CBHW060633030426
42337CB00018B/3334